e f g h i

n o p q r

w x y z

This edition published in 2001 by Brimax
First published in Great Britain in 1997 by Brimax
an imprint of Octopus Publishing Group Ltd
2-4 Heron Quays, London, E14 4JP

My First Dictionary

BRIMAX

Aa

acrobat

Morris thinks the **acrobat** is very clever.

alligator

The **alligator** has very sharp teeth.

alphabet

Katie can say her **alphabet**.

ambulance

The **ambulance** takes Daisy to the hospital.

ape

The **ape** is hanging upside-down.

apple

Cool Dog picks an **apple** from the tree.

apron

Foxy wears an **apron** to do the dishes.

armchair

Morris is asleep in the **armchair**.

arrow

Katie is lost so she follows the **arrow**.

astronaut

Wise Owl wishes he could fly as high as an **astronaut**.

axe

Foxy chops wood with an **axe**.

Bb

bag

Daisy takes her books to school in a **bag**.

ball

Cool Dog hits the **ball** as hard as he can.

balloon

Morris lets go of the **balloon**. It floats away.

banana

Katie eats a **banana**.

bandage

The nurse puts a **bandage** on Daisy's leg.

bat

Cool Dog has a baseball **bat**.

bath tub

There are too many bubbles in Foxy's **bath tub**.

7

beach

Wise Owl finds a shell on the **beach**.

bed

Katie is asleep in her **bed**.

bee

The **bee** flies from flower to flower.

bell

Daisy rings the **bell**.

bench

Morris and Cool Dog sit on the **bench**.

bicycle

Foxy's **bicycle** is red.

big

An elephant is **big**.

bird

Wise Owl is a **bird**.

birthday

It is Katie's **birthday**. She has some presents.

blackboard

Cool Dog draws on the **blackboard**.

blocks

Foxy builds a house with his **blocks**.

blowing

Wise Owl is **blowing** out the candles on his cake.

blue

Daisy is wearing a **blue** dress.

boat

Morris is rowing the **boat**.

bone

The dog is burying a **bone**.

book

Katie puts a **book** on the shelf.

boots

Morris wears his **boots** to splash through a puddle.

bottle

Cool Dog buys a **bottle** of lemonade.

bottom

Daisy is at the **bottom** of the stairs.

branch

Wise Owl flies up and sits on the **branch**.

bread

Morris buys a loaf of **bread**.

breakfast

bridge

Katie has toast for **breakfast**.

Daisy walks over the **bridge**.

broom

brown

brush

Wise Owl sweeps the floor with the **broom**.

Cool Dog sees a **brown** bear at the zoo.

Katie's **brush** is on her dresser.

bubble

bucket

bush

Foxy is blowing a big **bubble**.

Morris fills a **bucket** with water.

Katie is hiding behind the **bush**.

butter

butterfly

button

Daisy likes to eat toast and **butter**.

A **butterfly** rests on the flower.

There is a **button** missing from Wise Owl's coat.

Cc

cake

Cool Dog eats a slice of **cake**.

camel

Foxy is riding a **camel**.

camera

Morris takes a photograph with his **camera**.

camping

Katie and Daisy are **camping** in the woods.

candle

There is a **candle** on Wise Owl's birthday cake.

cap

Cool Dog is wearing a **cap**.

car

Foxy's **car** is parked outside his house.

carpet

Katie's **carpet** is green.

carrot

Morris eats a **carrot**.

castle

Daisy thinks the **castle** looks spooky.

11

cat

The **cat** is cleaning her paws.

caterpillar

There is a **caterpillar** on Wise Owl's plant.

cave

Cool Dog sees a **cave** in the rocks.

chair

Foxy sits on a **chair**.

chalk

Katie writes her name on the blackboard with some **chalk**.

cheese

Morris loves to eat **cheese**.

chicken

The **chicken** has laid an egg.

chocolate

Daisy loves to eat **chocolate**.

climbing

Cool Dog is **climbing** a ladder.

clock

Foxy looks at the **clock** to see what time it is.

cloud

Morris can see one white **cloud** in the sky.

clown

The **clown** makes Katie laugh.

coat

Daisy wears a blue **coat**.

comb

Foxy uses a **comb** on his tail.

computer

Cool Dog is working on a **computer**.

cookie

Morris is eating a **cookie**.

cooking

Katie is **cooking** her dinner.

counting

Daisy is **counting** her money.

cow

The **cow** has a calf.

crab

Wise Owl finds a **crab** in the water.

13

crane

The **crane** is yellow.

crayon

Cool Dog's **crayon** is blue.

crocodile

The **crocodile** is in the water.

crown

Foxy is wearing a **crown**.

cup

Morris drinks a **cup** of coffee.

cupboard

Katie's **cupboard** is empty.

Dd

daffodil

There is a **daffodil** growing in Daisy's garden.

dancing

Cool Dog is **dancing** to some music.

deer

Wise Owl sees a **deer** in the forest.

dentist

The **dentist** is looking at Foxy's teeth.

desk

Morris is working at his **desk**.

diamond

Katie draws a **diamond**.

digging

Daisy is **digging** a hole.

dinosaur

A **dinosaur** is an animal that lived long ago.

doctor

The **doctor** takes Wise Owl's temperature.

dog

The **dog** is burying a bone.

dolphin

Cool Dog sees the **dolphin** jump out of the water.

donkey

Foxy feeds the **donkey** a carrot.

door

Morris opens the **door**.

dragon

Cool Dog paints a picture of a **dragon**.

drawer

Daisy puts some clothes in a **drawer**.

drawing

Wise Owl is **drawing** a picture.

dress

Katie is wearing a new **dress**.

drink

Foxy is thirsty. He has a **drink**.

driving

Morris is **driving** his car.

drum

Katie is banging on the **drum**.

dry

It is raining but Daisy is **dry**.

duck

The **duck** is swimming on the pond.

Ee

eagle

The **eagle** can fly very high.

ear

Cool Dog points to his **ear**.

eating

Foxy is **eating** an apple.

egg

The chicken has laid an **egg**.

elbow

Morris points to his **elbow**.

elephant

The **elephant** sprays water at Katie.

empty

Daisy's cupboard is **empty**.

envelope

Wise Owl puts a letter in the **envelope**.

eye

Cool Dog points to his **eye**.

Ff

fairy

There is a **fairy** in Foxy's book.

farm

Morris likes to visit the **farm**.

fast

feather

Katie is running very **fast**.

There is a **feather** in Daisy's hat.

feet

fence

field

Wise Owl has ticklish **feet**.

Cool Dog is painting the **fence**.

Foxy can see some cows in the **field**.

fish

flag

The **fish** are swimming all around.

Morris is waving a **flag**.

flower

foot

forest

Katie's **flower** is yellow.

Daisy has hurt her **foot**.

Wise Owl is flying through the **forest**.

fork

Cool Dog is holding a **fork**.

fountain

Foxy is taking a photograph of the **fountain**.

fox

Foxy is a **fox**.

frog

The **frog** is green.

full

Katie's cupboard is **full** of food.

Gg

garage

Morris parks his car in the **garage**.

garden

There are flowers in Daisy's **garden**.

gate

Wise Owl opens the **gate**.

ghost

Cool Dog sees a **ghost**.

giant

Foxy reads a story about a **giant**.

giraffe

The **giraffe** has a very long neck.

glass

Morris drinks a **glass** of milk.

glasses

Katie is wearing **glasses**.

glove

Daisy can only find one **glove**.

goat

The **goat** is eating Wise Owl's flowers.

goldfish

Cool Dog has a **goldfish**.

goose

Foxy feeds the **goose**.

grass

Morris is cutting the **grass**.

green

Katie's front door is **green**.

guitar

Daisy can play the **guitar**.

Hh

hammer

Wise Owl hits the nail with a **hammer**.

hand

Cool Dog waves his **hand**.

handkerchief

Foxy blows his nose on a **handkerchief**.

hanging

Morris is **hanging** up his coat.

hat

Katie is wearing a **hat**.

head

A butterfly lands on Daisy's **head**.

heavy

Wise Owl's bag is **heavy**.

helicopter

Cool Dog can see a **helicopter**.

hiding

Foxy is **hiding** behind the door.

hill

Morris is at the top of the **hill**.

hippopotamus

The **hippopotamus** is very big.

hole

There is a **hole** in Daisy's sock.

hook

Cool Dog hangs his coat on the **hook**.

hoop

Foxy plays with a **hoop**.

hopping

Morris is **hopping** on one leg.

hopscotch

Katie is playing **hopscotch**.

horse

Daisy is riding a **horse**.

hose

Wise Owl cleans his car with a **hose**.

hospital

Cool Dog is visiting a friend in the **hospital**.

house

This is Foxy's **house**.

Ii

ice cream

Morris is eating **ice cream**.

ice skates

Katie puts her **ice skates** on.

icicle

There is an **icicle** hanging from Daisy's roof.

igloo

Wise Owl and Cool Dog build an **igloo**.

inside

Foxy is **inside** his house.

iron

Morris uses an **iron** to iron his clothes.

island

Katie rows across to the **island**.

Jj

jacket

Daisy is wearing a blue **jacket**.

jack-in-the-box

The **jack-in-the-box** gives Wise Owl a fright.

jar

Cool Dog puts the **jar** on the table.

jeans

Foxy is wearing some **jeans**.

jigsaw puzzle

Morris has finished the **jigsaw puzzle**.

jug

Daisy fills the **jug** with milk.

jumping

Cool Dog is **jumping** over a fence.

jungle

Wise Owl is in the **jungle**.

Kk

kangaroo

The **kangaroo** has a baby in its pouch.

key

Foxy unlocks the door with his **key**.

kicking

Morris is **kicking** a ball.

kid

A baby goat is called a **kid**.

king

A **king** wears a crown. Wise Owl pretends to be a **king**.

kitchen

Katie is cooking in the **kitchen**.

kite

Daisy is flying a **kite**.

kitten

Wise Owl's **kitten** is very playful.

knee

Cool Dog has hurt his **knee**.

knife

Foxy cuts the cake with a **knife**.

knot

Morris ties a **knot** in the rope.

koala

The **koala** is in the tree.

Ll

ladder

Katie climbs the **ladder**.

lamp

Daisy turns the **lamp** on.

laughing

Wise Owl is **laughing** at the clown.

leaf

Cool Dog picks up a **leaf**.

leg

Foxy hops on one **leg**.

leopard

The **leopard** is sleeping.

letter

Morris writes a **letter** to his friend.

lettuce

Katie is eating some **lettuce**.

licking

Daisy is **licking** a lollipop.

light

Wise Owl's bag is empty. It is very **light**.

lighthouse

Cool Dog climbs right to the top of the **lighthouse**.

lightning

Foxy watches the **lightning** from the window.

lion

The **lion** roars very loudly.

little

Morris eats the **little** cookie. He saves the big cookie for later.

Mm

map

Katie looks at the **map**. She is lost.

marbles

Daisy is playing with some **marbles**.

medal

Wise Owl wins the race. He is given a **medal**.

medicine

Cool Dog is ill. He has to take some **medicine**.

mermaid

There is a picture of a **mermaid** in Foxy's book.

merry-go-round

Morris is on the **merry-go-round**.

microwave

Katie puts some food in the **microwave**.

milk

Daisy drinks some **milk**.

mirror

Wise Owl looks at himself in the **mirror**.

mittens

Foxy is wearing red **mittens**.

mixing bowl

Morris is making a cake. He puts flour into a **mixing bowl**.

money

Katie puts some **money** in her piggy bank.

moon

Daisy can see the **moon** through the window.

mountain

Wise Owl wants to climb a **mountain**.

mouse

There is a **mouse** in Cool Dog's kitchen.

mushroom

Foxy is eating a **mushroom**.

Nn

nail

Morris hits the **nail** with a hammer.

neck

Katie wears a scarf around her **neck**.

necklace

Daisy is wearing a **necklace**.

needle

Wise Owl is sewing with a **needle** and thread.

nest

There are three eggs in the **nest**.

net

Cool Dog catches a fish in his **net**.

newspaper

Foxy is reading the **newspaper**.

nose

Morris points to his **nose**.

nurse

The **nurse** takes Katie's temperature.

nut

Daisy is eating a **nut**.

oar

Wise Owl uses an **oar** to row the boat.

octopus

An **octopus** has eight arms.

onion

Cool Dog is slicing an **onion**.

orange

Foxy is eating an **orange**.

orchard

Morris is picking apples in the **orchard.**

orchestra

Katie plays the violin in the **orchestra**.

organ

Daisy can play the **organ**.

oven

Cool Dog puts a cake in the **oven**.

owl

Wise Owl is an **owl**.

Pp

painting

Foxy is **painting** a picture.

panda

A **panda** is black and white.

park

Morris is at the **park**.

parrot

"Hello, Katie," says the **parrot**.

party

Daisy is having a birthday **party**.

path

Wise Owl walks up the **path**.

pencil

Cool Dog is writing with a **pencil**.

penguin

Foxy likes to watch the **penguin**.

piano

Morris can play the **piano**.

picnic

Katie and Daisy are having a **picnic**.

picture

Wise Owl paints a **picture**.

pig

A **pig** has a curly tail.

pillow

Cool Dog lays his head on the **pillow**.

pineapple

Foxy buys a **pineapple**.

pink

Katie is wearing a **pink** hat.

plane

Morris can see a **plane** in the sky.

plate

Daisy puts the **plate** in the cupboard.

polar bear

The **polar bear** eats a fish.

pond

There are fish in Wise Owl's **pond**.

pony

Cool Dog feeds the **pony** a carrot.

potato

Foxy is peeling a **potato**.

present

Morris gives a birthday **present** to Katie.

puddle

Daisy splashes in the **puddle**.

pulling

Wise Owl is **pulling** his toboggan through the snow.

puppy

The **puppy** is chewing Cool Dog's slipper.

purple

Foxy's hat is **purple**.

purse

Katie keeps her money in her **purse**.

pushing

Morris is **pushing** the wheelbarrow.

Qq

queen

Daisy dreams that she is a **queen**.

question mark

Wise Owl draws a **question mark** on the blackboard.

quilt

Cool Dog is asleep under the **quilt**.

Rr

rabbit

The **rabbit** is eating a carrot.

radio

Foxy is listening to the **radio**.

raft

Morris has built a **raft**.

rain

Katie is outside in the **rain**.

rainbow

Daisy can see a **rainbow**.

reading

Wise Owl is **reading** a book.

red

Cool Dog is painting the fence **red**.

refrigerator

Foxy puts the milk in the **refrigerator**.

rhinoceros

A **rhinoceros** has a big horn.

ribbon

Katie puts a **ribbon** around her neck.

ring

Daisy is wearing a **ring**.

river

Wise Owl is fishing in the **river**.

robin

There is a **robin** outside Cool Dog's window.

robot

The **robot** can walk and talk.

rocket

Foxy watches as the **rocket** shoots into the sky.

rocking chair

Morris is sitting on the **rocking chair**.

rocking horse

Katie is playing on the **rocking horse**.

roller skates

Daisy is putting on her **roller skates**.

rolling

The ball is **rolling** down the hill.

roof

Wise Owl has flown onto the **roof**.

rope

Cool Dog is swinging on a **rope**.

rose

Foxy is smelling the **rose**.

rug

Morris has a **rug** in front of the fire.

running

Katie is **running** as fast as she can.

Ss

sandcastle

Daisy has built a **sandcastle**.

saucepan

Wise Owl puts the **saucepan** in the cupboard.

scarecrow

Cool Dog puts a hat on the **scarecrow**.

scarf

It is cold. Foxy is wearing a **scarf**.

school

Morris is at **school**.

scissors

Katie cuts some paper with **scissors**.

scooter

Daisy is riding a **scooter**.

sea

Cool Dog is swimming in the **sea**.

sea gull

A **sea gull** is sitting on Wise Owl's fence.

seal

The **seal** is playing with a ball.

see-saw

Foxy and Morris are on the **see-saw**.

sheet

Katie puts a clean **sheet** on her bed.

shelf

Daisy puts some books on the **shelf**.

shell

Wise Owl finds a **shell** on the beach.

ship

Cool Dog can see a **ship** sailing past.

shoe

Foxy can find only one **shoe**.

shovel

Morris is digging with a **shovel.**

sitting

Katie is **sitting** on a chair.

skateboard

Daisy is playing on her **skateboard**.

skating

Wise Owl is **skating** round and round.

skiing

Cool Dog is **skiing** in the snow.

skipping

Foxy is **skipping**.

skirt

Katie is wearing a **skirt**.

slide

Morris is at the top of the **slide**.

slippers

Daisy is wearing her **slippers**.

slow

The tortoise is very **slow**.

| A | B | C | D | E | F | G | H | I | J | K | L | M | N | O | P | Q | R | **S** | T | U | V | W | X | Y | Z |
| a | b | c | d | e | f | g | h | i | j | k | l | m | n | o | p | q | r | **s** | t | u | v | w | x | y | z |

snail

Wise Owl sees a **snail** on the path.

snow

Cool Dog is playing in the **snow**.

snowball

Foxy throws a **snowball** at Morris.

snowman

Katie and Daisy have built a **snowman**.

soap

Wise Owl washes his face with **soap**.

sock

Cool Dog has one red **sock**.

spider

The **spider** is in the middle of its web.

splashing

Foxy is **splashing** through the puddles.

sponge

Morris uses a **sponge** to wash his car.

spoon

Katie eats some yogurt with a **spoon**.

standing

Daisy is **standing** up.

star

Wise Owl can see a **star** in the sky.

starfish

Cool Dog finds a **starfish** on the beach.

stethoscope

The doctor listens to Foxy's heart with his **stethoscope**.

stirring

Morris is **stirring** the cake mix.

stool

Katie is sitting on a **stool**.

straw

Daisy is drinking her lemonade through a **straw**.

sun

The **sun** is shining very brightly.

swimming

Cool Dog is **swimming** in a race.

swing

Wise Owl is playing on a **swing**.

Tt

table

Morris is sitting at the **table**.

tail

Foxy has a bushy **tail**.

teacher

The **teacher** tells Katie to write her name on the paper.

teddy bear

Daisy takes her **teddy bear** to bed with her.

telephone

Wise Owl is talking to his friend on the **telephone**.

television

Cool Dog is watching the **television.**

tent

Foxy is camping in a **tent.**

thermometer

The nurse takes Katie's temperature with a **thermometer**.

throwing

Morris is **throwing** a ball.

tie

Wise Owl is wearing a **tie**.

tiger

Daisy thinks the **tiger** is very fierce.

toad

There is a **toad** in Foxy's pond.

toboggan

Morris is sliding down the hill in his **toboggan**.

40

tomato

Katie is eating a **tomato**.

toolbox

Daisy is looking for a hammer in her **toolbox**.

toothbrush

Cool Dog cleans his teeth with his **toothbrush**.

towel

Wise Owl dries himself with a **towel**.

tower

Foxy has climbed to the top of the **tower**.

toy box

Morris has a blue **toy box**.

toys

Morris puts his **toys** into the toy box.

tractor

Katie has a ride on the big, blue **tractor**.

train

Daisy is riding at the front of the **train**.

trampoline

Wise Owl can bounce very high on the **trampoline**.

tree

Cool Dog is climbing the **tree**.

trousers

Foxy is wearing green **trousers**.

truck

There is a **truck** outside Katie's house.

trumpet

Morris can play the **trumpet**.

t-shirt

Daisy is wearing a yellow **t-shirt**.

tunnel

The train goes through the **tunnel**.

turkey

Cool Dog sees a **turkey** on the farm.

typewriter

Wise Owl is typing a letter on his **typewriter**.

Uu

umbrella

Foxy's **umbrella** is red, yellow and blue.

unicorn

There is a picture of a **unicorn** in Katie's book.

uniform

Morris has dressed up in a soldier's **uniform**.

Vv

vacuum cleaner

Daisy is cleaning the carpet with the **vacuum cleaner**.

van

Wise Owl is driving a **van**.

vase

Cool Dog puts some flowers in a **vase**.

violin

Foxy can play the **violin**.

vulture

Morris sees a **vulture** in a tree.

Ww

wall

There is a bird sitting on the **wall**.

washing

Katie is **washing** her car.

wave

Wise Owl jumps over the **wave**.

wet

Cool Dog has lost his umbrella. He is very **wet**.

wheel

The **wheel** has fallen off Foxy's bike.

wheelbarrow

Morris pushes the **wheelbarrow** up the path.

wheelchair

Katie has hurt her leg. She has to use a **wheelchair**.

whistle

Daisy is blowing a **whistle**.

windmill

Wise Owl can see a **windmill**.

window

Cool Dog is looking out of the **window**.

witch

A **witch** rides along on a broomstick.

writing

Foxy is **writing** a letter.

Xx

x-ray

Morris is having an **x-ray**.

xylophone

Katie is playing the **xylophone**.

Yy

yard

Wise Owl sits out in his **yard**.

yellow

Cool Dog has a **yellow** car.

yogurt

Foxy is eating some **yogurt**.

yo-yo

Morris is playing with a **yo-yo**.

Zz

zebra

A **zebra** has black and white stripes.

zig-zag

Katie draws a **zig-zag** on the blackboard.

zipper

Daisy fastens the **zipper** on her jacket.

zoo

There are lots of animals at the **zoo**.

a b c d

j k l m

s t u v